easy meals

Low Fat

p

This is a Parragon Book
First printed in 2001

Parragon
Queen Street House
4 Queen Street
Bath BA1 1HE
United Kingdom

ISBN: 0-75255-767-X

Printed in Spain

Produced by The Bridgewater Book Company Ltd, Lewes, East Sussex

Creative Director Terry Jeavons
Art Director Sarah Howerd
Page Make-up Sara Kidd
Editorial Director Fiona Biggs
Senior Editor Mark Truman
Editorial Assistant Tom Kitch

NOTES FOR THE READER

- This book uses both metric and imperial measurements. Follow the same units of measurement throughout; do not mix metric and imperial.
- All spoon measurements are level: teaspoons are assumed to be 5 ml, and table-spoons are assumed to be 15 ml.
- Unless otherwise stated, milk is assumed to be full-fat, eggs and individual vegetables such as potatoes are medium-sized, and pepper is freshly ground black pepper.
- Recipes using raw or very lightly cooked eggs should be avoided by infants, the elderly, pregnant women, convalescents, and anyone suffering from an illness.
- Optional ingredients, variations, and serving suggestions have not been included in the calculations.
- The times given are an approximate guide only. Preparation times differ according to the techniques used by different people and the cooking times vary as a result of the type of oven used.

Contents

Introduction

Changing your diet to lower its fat content may sound like a
a challenge, but it will not be difficult if you adopt a positive
attitude. You simply need to adjust your cooking methods and
make use of some of the inspiring recipe ideas in this book. All
the dishes are easy to prepare and cook, so you will not need to
resort to unhealthy fast food even when time is short, as on mid-
week evenings. The recipes have been gathered from cultures
ranging from Thai, Chinese and Indian to Mediterranean and
Mexican – so you may find yourself trying out exciting new ideas
as well as cutting down on cholesterol. This lifestyle change will
not leave you feeling disadvantaged.

The recipes rely heavily on ingredients which are naturally low in
fat, such as fish, chicken, lean cuts of meat, fresh vegetables,
beans, and foods such as pasta which are high in energy-giving
carbohydrates. They also use reduced-fat milk, yogurt, cheese
and margarine, all of which are readily available. Butter does not

guide to recipe key	
easy	Recipes are graded as follows: 1 pea = easy; 2 peas = very easy; 3 peas = extremely easy.
serves 4	Most of the recipes in this book serve four people. Simply halve the ingredients to serve two, taking care not to mix imperial and metric measurements.
15 minutes	Preparation time. Where recipes include marinating, soaking, standing, or chilling, times for these are listed separately: eg, 15 minutes, plus 30 minutes to marinate.
15 minutes	Cooking time. Cooking times do not include the cooking of rice or noodles served with the main dishes.

appear, but olive oil – an essential ingredient in the healthy Mediterranean diet – is included in small amounts. The recipes also make good use of flavourings and seasonings. A dish can be transformed with fresh, fragrant herbs, hot chillies, pungent garlic, zesty ginger root, and warming spices.

Dinner parties and weekend brunches and lunches are times when you may feel inclined to indulge in fatty foods. Instead, devote extra time to planning a special menu. Vietnamese Rice Paper Wraps, followed by Beef & Peppers with Lemon Grass and a Lychee & Ginger Sorbet is one suggestion for turning a low-fat meal into a gastronomic occasion.

Chicken & Mango Stir-Fry, page 30

Soups & Starters

It is very easy to create a low-fat starter. Simple soups are an obvious first choice. Made simply from vegetables, beans, lean meat or fish cooked in stock, they may still be impressive if exotically flavoured and garnished. Alternatively, use fruit or raw vegetable juice. Cold Tomato, Carrot & Orange Soup is the ultimate healthy starter, entirely fat-free, and made from raw ingredients, so all the goodness is retained. For a more exotic, elegant appetiser, serve Lemon Grass Chicken Skewers. With skewers fashioned from lemon grass and a garnish of coriander and lime, they make a delicious talking point.

Sweet & Sour Cabbage Soup

INGREDIENTS

85 g/3 oz sultanas
125 ml/4 fl oz orange
 juice
1 tbsp olive oil
1 large onion, chopped
250 g/9 oz shredded
 cabbage
2 apples, peeled and
 diced
125 ml/4 fl oz apple juice
400 g/14 oz canned
 peeled tomatoes in
 juice
225 ml/8 fl oz tomato or
 vegetable juice
100 g/3½ oz pineapple
 flesh, chopped finely
1.2 litres/2 pints water
2 tsp wine vinegar
salt and pepper
fresh mint leaves,
 to garnish

❶ Put the sultanas in a bowl, pour the orange juice over them, and leave for 15 minutes.

❷ Heat the oil in a large saucepan over a medium heat, add the onion, cover, and cook for 3–4 minutes, stirring frequently, until the onion starts to soften. Add the cabbage and cook for 2 minutes more; do not allow it to brown.

❸ Add the apples and apple juice, cover, and cook gently for 5 minutes. Stir in the tomatoes, tomato juice, pineapple and water. Season with salt and pepper and add the vinegar.

❹ Add the sultanas and the orange juice. Bring to the boil, reduce the heat and simmer, partially covered, for about 1 hour, or until the fruit and vegetables are tender.

❺ Let the soup cool slightly, then transfer to a blender or a food processor and purée until smooth; work in batches if necessary. (If using a food processor, strain off the liquid and reserve. Purée the soup solids with enough liquid to moisten them, then combine with the remaining liquid.)

❻ Return the soup to the saucepan and simmer gently for about 10 minutes to reheat. Ladle into warm bowls. Garnish with mint leaves and serve immediately.

 easy

 serves 4

20 minutes,
plus 15 minutes
to soak raisins

 1½ hours

Fennel & Tomato Soup with Prawns

INGREDIENTS

2 tsp olive oil
1 large onion, halved and
    sliced
2 large fennel bulbs,
    halved and sliced
1 small potato, diced
850 ml/1½ pints water
400 ml/14 fl oz tomato
    juice
1 bay leaf
125 g/4½ oz cooked
    peeled small prawns
2 tomatoes, skinned,
    deseeded and
    chopped
½ tsp snipped fresh dill
salt and pepper
dill sprigs or fennel
    fronds, to garnish

❶ Heat the olive oil in a large saucepan over a medium heat. Add the onion and fennel and cook for 3–4 minutes, stirring occasionally, until the onion is just softened.

❷ Add the potato, water, tomato juice and bay leaf, and a large pinch of salt. Reduce the heat, cover, and simmer for about 25 minutes, stirring once or twice, until the vegetables are soft.

❸ Allow the mixture to cool slightly, then transfer it to a blender or a food processor and purée until the soup is smooth, working in batches if necessary. (If using a food processor, strain off the cooking liquid and reserve. Purée the soup solids with enough cooking liquid to moisten them, then combine with the remaining liquid.)

❹ Return the soup to the saucepan and add the prawns. Simmer gently for about 10 minutes to reheat the soup and allow it to absorb the prawn flavour.

❺ Stir in the tomatoes and dill. Taste and add salt and pepper, if needed. If the soup seems too thick, thin it with a little more tomato juice. Ladle into warm bowls, garnish with dill or fennel fronds, and serve hot.

easy

serves 4

20 minutes

50 minutes

Oriental Pork Balls & Greens in Broth

INGREDIENTS

2 litres/3½ pints chicken
   stock
85 g/3 oz shiitake
   mushrooms, thinly
   sliced
175 g/6 oz pak choi or
   other oriental greens,
   sliced into thin
   ribbons
6 spring onions, finely
   sliced
salt and pepper

PORK BALLS
225 g/8 oz lean minced
   pork
25 g/1 oz fresh spinach
   leaves, chopped finely
2 spring onions,
   chopped finely
1 garlic clove, chopped
   very finely
pinch of 5-spice powder
1 tsp soy sauce

❶ To make the pork balls, put the pork, spinach, spring onions and garlic in a bowl. Add the 5-spice powder and soy sauce and mix until combined.

❷ Shape the pork mixture into 24 balls. Place them in one layer in a steamer that will fit over the top of a saucepan.

❸ Bring the stock just to the boil in a saucepan that will accommodate the steamer. Regulate the heat so that the liquid bubbles gently. Add the mushrooms to the stock and place the steamer, covered, on top of the pan. Steam for 10 minutes. Remove the steamer and set aside on a plate.

❹ Add the pak choi and spring onions to the pan and cook gently in the stock for 3–4 minutes, or until the leaves are wilted. Taste the soup and adjust the seasoning, if necessary.

❺ Divide the pork balls evenly among 6 warm bowls and ladle the soup over them. Serve at once.

 very easy

 makes 24

 20 minutes

 15 minutes

Greek Bean Soup with Lemon & Mint

INGREDIENTS

1 tbsp olive oil
1 large onion, chopped
finely
1 large carrot, diced
finely
2 celery sticks, chopped
finely
4 tomatoes, skinned,
deseeded and
chopped, or 250 g/
9 oz drained canned
tomatoes
2 garlic cloves, chopped
finely
800 g/1 lb 12 oz canned
cannellini or haricot
beans, drained and
rinsed well
1.2 litres/2 pints water
1 courgette, finely diced
grated rind of ½ lemon
1 tbsp chopped fresh
mint, or ¼ tsp dried
mint
1 tsp chopped fresh
thyme, or ⅛ tsp dried
thyme
1 bay leaf
400 g/14 oz canned
artichoke hearts
salt and pepper

❶ Heat 1 teaspoon of the olive oil in a large saucepan over a medium heat. Add the onion and cook for 3–4 minutes, stirring occasionally, until the onion softens. Add the carrot, celery, tomatoes and garlic, and continue cooking for 5 minutes more, stirring frequently.

❷ Add the beans and water. Bring to the boil, reduce the heat, cover, and cook gently for about 10 minutes.

❸ Add the courgette, lemon rind, mint, thyme and bay leaf, and season with salt and pepper. Cover and simmer for about 40 minutes, or until all the vegetables are tender. Allow to cool slightly. Transfer 450 ml/16 fl oz to a blender or a food processor, purée until smooth, and recombine.

❹ Meanwhile, heat the remaining oil in a frying pan over a medium heat, adding more if necessary to coat the bottom of the pan. Fry the artichokes, cut side down, until lightly browned. Turn over and fry long enough to heat through.

❺ Ladle the soup into warm bowls and top each with an artichoke heart.

 easy

 serves 4

 20 minutes

 1 hour

Cold Tomato, Carrot & Orange Soup

INGREDIENTS

3 large seedless oranges
4 ripe tomatoes
2 celery sticks, strings
    removed, chopped
3 carrots, grated
350 ml/12 fl oz
    tomato juice
salt
Tabasco sauce (optional)
1 tbsp chopped fresh
    mint
fresh mint sprigs, to
    garnish

❶ Working over a bowl to catch the juices, peel the oranges. Cut down between the membranes and drop the orange segments into the bowl.

❷ Put the tomatoes in a small bowl and pour boiling water over to cover them. Leave them to stand for 10 seconds, then drain. Peel off the skin and cut the tomatoes in half crossways. Scoop out the seeds into a sieve set over a bowl. Reserve the tomato juices.

❸ Put the tomatoes, celery and carrots in a blender (or food processor). Add the orange segments and their juice and the juice saved from the tomatoes. Purée until smooth.

❹ Scrape into a bowl and stir in the tomato juice. Cover and chill until cold.

❺ Taste the soup and add salt and a few drops of Tabasco sauce if necessary to intensify the flavour, if wished. Stir in the chopped mint, ladle the soup into cold bowls, and garnish with fresh mint sprigs.

 very easy

 serves 24

15–20 minutes

16 minutes

COOK'S TIP
This soup really needs to be made in a blender for the best texture. A food processor can be used, but the soup will not be completely smooth.

Griddled Smoked Salmon

INGREDIENTS

350 g/12 oz sliced
  smoked salmon
1 tsp Dijon mustard
1 garlic clove, crushed
2 tsp chopped fresh dill
2 tsp sherry vinegar
4 tbsp olive oil
115 g/4 oz mixed salad
  leaves
salt and pepper

❶ Take the slices of smoked salmon and fold them, making two folds accordion-style, so they form little parcels.

❷ Whisk the mustard, garlic, dill, vinegar and seasoning together. Gradually whisk in the olive oil to form a light emulsion.

❸ Heat a ridged griddle until it smokes. Cook the salmon bundles on one side only for 2–3 minutes, or until they are heated through and marked from the pan.

❹ Meanwhile, dress the salad leaves with some of the vinaigrette and divide them between 4 serving plates. Top with the cooked smoked salmon, cooked side up. Drizzle with the remaining dressing.

 extremely easy

 serves 4

 5 minutes

 2–3 minutes

Vietnamese Rice Paper Wraps

INGREDIENTS

225 g/8 oz cooked
   peeled prawns
225 g/8 oz salmon fillet,
   seared for 1 minute
   each side and cut into
   5 mm/¼ inch slices
225 g/8 oz tuna steak,
   seared for 1 minute
   each side and cut into
   5 mm/¼ inch slices
2 ripe avocados, peeled,
   sliced and sprinkled
   with lime juice
6–8 asparagus tips,
   blanched
1 small red onion, thinly
   sliced
16 spring onions, sliced
12 black Niçoise olives,
   sliced
14 cherry tomatoes,
   halved
large bunch of coriander,
   leaves stripped from
   the stems
20–30 rice paper
   wrappers, preferably
   18 cm/7 inch rounds
lime wedges

❶ To make the dipping sauces, put the ingredients for each into separate bowls and stir together to blend.

❷ Arrange the prawns, fish, vegetables and coriander leaves on a large serving plate in groups, ready to use as different fillings for the wrappers. Cover loosely with cling film and chill until ready to serve.

❸ Dip each wrapper very briefly into a bowl of warm water to soften it. Lay the wrappers on clean tea towels to absorb any excess water, then pile them onto a serving plate and cover with a damp tea towel.

❹ To serve, let the guests fill their own wrappers. Offer lime wedges for squeezing over the fillings, and pass the dipping sauces around separately.

SPICED VINEGAR DIPPING SAUCE
80 ml/3 fl oz rice vinegar
2 tbsp Thai fish sauce
2 tbsp caster sugar
1 garlic clove, chopped finely
2 red chillies, deseeded and thinly
   sliced
2 tbsp chopped fresh coriander

SOY DIPPING SAUCE
125 ml/4 fl oz Thai fish sauce
4–6 tbsp lime juice
2 tbsp Japanese soy sauce
2–3 tbsp light brown sugar
2.5 cm/1 inch piece fresh ginger root,
   chopped finely
2–4 garlic cloves, crushed

 extremely easy

 serves 4

 25–30 minutes

 5 minutes

Lemon Grass Chicken Skewers

INGREDIENTS

2 long or 4 short stalks
of lemon grass
2 large boneless,
skinless chicken
breasts (halves),
about 400 g/14 oz in
total
1 small egg white
1 carrot, finely grated
1 small red chilli,
deseeded and
chopped
2 tbsp fresh garlic chives,
chopped
2 tbsp fresh coriander,
chopped
1 tbsp sunflower oil
salt and pepper
coriander and lime slices,
to garnish

1 If the lemon grass stalks are long, cut them in half across the middle to make 4 short lengths. Cut each stalk in half lengthways, so you have 8 sticks.

2 Roughly chop the chicken pieces and place them in a food processor with the egg white. Process to a smooth paste, then add the carrot, chilli, chives, coriander, and salt and pepper. Process for a few seconds to mix well.

3 Chill the mixture in the refrigerator for about 15 minutes. Divide the mixture into 8 equal portions, and use your hands to shape the mixture around the skewers fashioned from lemon grass.

4 Brush the skewers with oil and grill under a preheated medium-hot grill for 4–6 minutes, turning them occasionally, until golden brown and thoroughly cooked. Alternatively, barbecue them over medium-hot coals.

5 Serve the chicken skewers hot, garnished with coriander and slices of lime.

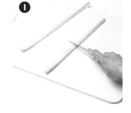

very easy

makes 8

20 minutes,
plus 15 minutes
to chill

4–6 minutes

Main
Meals

Stir-frying is an excellent way of cooking meat, fish and vegetables in the minimum of fat. It is also a fast cooking method, so you may take only minutes to make an attractive dish that tastes sensational. There are several great ideas for stir-fries in this part of the book. Try the Sauté of Chicken, Corn & Mangetouts for a mix of flavours combined with interesting texture. Steaming is the ideal cooking method for a healthy, low-fat diet. Steamed Yellow Fish Fillets, spicy and colourful, are an unusual and lower fat alternative to battered, fried fish.

Beef & Peppers with Lemon Grass

INGREDIENTS

500 g/1 lb 2 oz lean beef
  fillet
2 tbsp vegetable oil
1 garlic clove, chopped
  finely
1 lemon grass stalk,
  finely shredded
2.5 cm/1 inch piece fresh
  ginger root, chopped
  finely
1 red pepper, deseeded
  and thickly sliced
1 green pepper,
  deseeded and thickly
  sliced
1 onion, thickly sliced
2 tbsp lime juice
boiled noodles or rice,
  to serve

❶ Cut the beef into long, thin strips, cutting across the grain.

❷ Heat the oil in a large frying pan or wok over a high heat. Add the garlic and stir-fry for 1 minute.

❸ Add the beef and stir-fry for an additional 2–3 minutes, or until lightly coloured. Stir in the lemon grass and ginger, and remove the wok from the heat.

❹ Remove the beef from the pan or wok and keep to one side. Next, add the peppers and onion to the pan or wok and stir-fry over a high heat for 2–3 minutes, or until the onions are just turning golden brown and slightly softened.

❺ Return the beef to the pan, stir in the lime juice, and season to taste with salt and pepper. Serve with noodles or rice, garnished with a flower made by cutting a red chilli.

 extremely easy

 serves 4

 15 minutes

 15 minutes

Roasted Red Pork

INGREDIENTS

600 g/1 lb 5 oz pork
    fillets
Chinese leaves,
    shredded to serve
red chilli flower, to
    garnish

MARINADE
2 garlic cloves, crushed
1 tbsp ginger root, grated
1 tbsp light soy sauce
1 tbsp Thai fish sauce
1 tbsp rice wine
1 tbsp hoi-sin sauce
1 tbsp sesame oil
1 tbsp palm sugar or soft
    brown sugar
½ tsp five-spice powder
a few drops red food
    colouring (optional)

extremely easy

serves 4

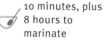
10 minutes, plus
8 hours to
marinate

1 hour

❶ Mix all the ingredients for the marinade together and spread the mixture over the pork, turning to coat evenly. Place in a large dish, cover, and leave in the refrigerator to marinate overnight.

❷ Place a rack in a roasting tin, then half-fill the tin with boiling water. Lift the pork from the marinade and place on the rack. Reserve the marinade for later use.

❸ Roast in a preheated oven at 220°C/425°F/Gas Mark 7 for 20 minutes. Baste with the marinade, lower the heat to 180°C/350°F/Gas Mark 4, and continue roasting for 35–40 minutes, basting occasionally with the marinade, until the pork is a rich reddish brown and cooked thoroughly.

❹ Cut the pork into slices and serve them on a bed of shredded Chinese leaves, garnished with a flower made by cutting a red chilli lengthways to form petals.

COOK'S TIP
The pork may also be grilled. Cut the meat into slices or strips and coat in the marinade. Arrange on a foil-lined grill pan and grill under a high heat, turning occasionally and basting with marinade.

Chicken & Mango Stir-Fry

INGREDIENTS

6 boneless, skinless
    chicken thighs
2.5 cm/1 inch piece fresh
    ginger root, grated
1 garlic clove, crushed
1 small red chilli,
    deseeded
1 large red pepper
4 spring onions
200 g/7 oz mangetouts
100 g/3½ oz baby
    sweetcorn cobs
1 large, firm, ripe mango
2 tbsp sunflower oil
1 tbsp light soy sauce
3 tbsp rice wine or sherry
1 tsp sesame oil
salt and pepper
sliced chives, to garnish

❶ Cut the chicken into long, thin strips and place them in a bowl. Mix together the ginger, garlic and chilli, then stir into the chicken strips to coat them evenly.

❷ Slice the pepper thinly, cutting diagonally. Trim the spring onions and slice them diagonally. Cut the mangetouts and the corn in half diagonally. Peel the mango, remove the stone, and slice thinly.

❸ Heat the oil in a large frying pan or wok over a high heat. Add the chicken thighs and stir-fry them for 4–5 minutes, or until they just turn golden brown. Add the peppers and stir-fry over a medium heat for 4–5 minutes to soften them.

❹ Add the spring onions, mangetouts and corn, and stir-fry for another minute.

❺ Mix together the soy sauce, rice wine or sherry, and the sesame oil and stir the mixture into the wok. Add the mango and stir gently for 1 minute to heat thoroughly.

❻ Adjust the seasoning with salt and pepper to taste and serve immediately. Garnish with chives.

 easy

 serves 4

 15 minutes

 15 minutes

Rice Noodles with Chicken & Chinese Leaves

INGREDIENTS

200 g/7 oz rice stick
  noodles
1 tbsp sunflower oil
1 garlic clove, chopped
  finely
2 cm/¾ inch piece fresh
  ginger root, chopped
  finely
4 spring onions, chopped
1 red bird-eye chilli,
  deseeded and sliced
300 g/10½ oz boneless,
  skinless chicken,
  chopped finely
2 chicken livers, chopped
  finely
1 celery stick, thinly sliced
1 carrot, cut into fine
  matchsticks
300 g/10½ oz shredded
  Chinese leaves
4 tbsp lime juice
2 tbsp Thai fish sauce
1 tbsp soy sauce

TO GARNISH
2 tbsp fresh mint,
  shredded
slices of pickled garlic
fresh mint sprig

❶ Soak the rice noodles in hot water for 15 minutes, or according to the package directions. Drain well.

❷ Heat the oil in a wok or a large frying pan and stir-fry the garlic, ginger, spring onions and chilli for about 1 minute. Stir in the chicken and chicken livers, then stir-fry over a high heat for 2–3 minutes or until the meat begins to brown.

❸ Stir in the celery and carrot, and stir-fry for 2 minutes to soften. Add the Chinese leaves, then stir in the lime juice, fish sauce and soy sauce.

❹ Add the noodles and stir to heat thoroughly. Sprinkle with shredded mint and pickled garlic. Serve immediately, garnished with a mint sprig.

 very easy

 serves 4

 15 minutes

 8 minutes

Chile Verde

INGREDIENTS

1 kg/2 lb 4 oz pork, cut
    into bite-sized chunks
1 onion, chopped
2 bay leaves
1 whole garlic bulb, cut
    in half
1 stock cube
2 garlic cloves, chopped
450 g/1 lb fresh
    tomatillos, husks
    removed, cooked in a
    small amount of water
    until just tender, then
    chopped
2 large fresh mild green
    chillies, such as anaheim,
    or a combination of
    1 green pepper and
    2 jalapeño chillies,
    deseeded and chopped
3 tbsp vegetable oil
225 ml/8 fl oz pork or
    chicken stock
½ tsp mild chilli powder,
    such as ancho or
    New Mexico
½ tsp cumin
4–6 tbsp chopped fresh
    coriander, to garnish

TO SERVE
warmed flour tortillas
lime wedges

❶ Place the pork in a large pan with the onion, bay leaves, garlic bulb and stock cube. Add water to cover and bring to the boil. Skim off the scum from the surface, reduce the heat to very low, and simmer gently for about 1½ hours, or until the meat is very tender.

❷ Meanwhile, put the chopped garlic in a blender or a food processor with the tomatillos and green chillies and pepper, if using. Process to a purée.

❸ Heat the oil in a pan, add the tomatillo mixture, and cook over a medium-high heat for about 10 minutes, or until thickened. Add the stock, chilli powder and cumin.

❹ When the meat is tender, remove it from the pan and add it to the sauce. Simmer gently to combine the flavours.

❺ Garnish with the chopped coriander and serve with warmed tortillas and lime wedges.

 easy

 serves 4

 10 minutes

 2¼ hours

Steamed Chicken & Vegetable Parcels

INGREDIENTS

4 boneless, skinless
   chicken breasts
1 tsp ground lemon grass
2 spring onions,
   chopped finely
250 g/9 oz young carrots
250 g/9 oz young
   courgettes
2 celery sticks
1 tsp light soy sauce
250 g/9 oz spinach
   leaves
2 tsp sesame oil
salt and pepper

❶ With a sharp knife, make a slit through one side of each chicken breast to open out a large pocket. Sprinkle the inside of the pocket with lemon grass, salt and pepper. Tuck the spring onions into the pockets.

❷ Trim the carrots, courgettes and celery, then cut into matchsticks. Plunge into a pan of boiling water for 1 minute, drain and toss in the soy sauce.

❸ Pack the vegetables into the pocket in each chicken breast and fold over firmly to enclose. Reserve any remaining vegetables. Wash the spinach leaves thoroughly, then drain and pat dry with kitchen paper. Wrap the chicken breasts firmly in the spinach leaves to enclose completely. If the leaves are too firm to wrap the chicken easily, steam them for a few seconds until they are softened and flexible.

❹ Place the wrapped chicken in a steamer and steam over rapidly boiling water for 20–25 minutes, depending on size.

❺ Stir-fry any leftover vegetable sticks and spinach for 1–2 minutes in the sesame oil, and serve with the chicken.

 easy

 serves 4

 25 minutes

 30 minutes

Italian Chicken Spirals

4 skinless, boneless
   chicken breasts
25 g/1 oz fresh basil
   leaves
15 g/½ oz hazelnuts
1 garlic clove, crushed
250 g/9 oz wholemeal
   pasta spirals
2 sun-dried tomatoes
   or fresh tomatoes
1 tbsp lemon juice
1 tbsp olive oil
1 tbsp capers
60 g/2¼ oz black olives
salt and pepper

❶ Beat the chicken breasts with a rolling pin to flatten them evenly.

❷ Place the basil and hazelnuts in a food processor and process until chopped finely. Mix with the garlic, salt and pepper.

❸ Spread the basil mixture over the chicken breasts and roll each one up from one short end to enclose the filling. Wrap each chicken roll tightly in foil so that it holds its shape, then seal the ends well.

❹ Bring a large pan of lightly salted water to the boil and cook the pasta until tender but still firm to the bite.

❺ Place the chicken parcels in a steamer basket or colander set over the pan, cover tightly, and steam for 10 minutes. Meanwhile, dice the tomatoes.

❻ Drain the pasta and return to the pan with the lemon juice, olive oil, tomatoes, capers and olives. Heat through.

❼ Pierce the chicken with a skewer to make sure that the juices run clear and not pink, then slice the chicken and arrange over the pasta. Serve immediately.

easy

serves 4

10 minutes

15 minutes

Sauté of Chicken, Corn & Mangetouts

INGREDIENTS

4 skinless, boneless
  chicken breasts
250 g/9 oz baby
  sweetcorn
250 g/9 oz mangetouts
2 tbsp sunflower oil
1 tbsp sherry vinegar
1 tbsp honey
1 tbsp light soy sauce
1 tbsp sunflower seeds
pepper
rice or egg noodles,
  to serve

❶ Using a sharp knife, slice the chicken breasts into long, thin strips. Cut the baby sweetcorn in half lengthways and top and tail the mangetouts. Set the vegetables aside until required.

❷ Heat the sunflower oil in a wok or a wide frying pan, and fry the chicken over a fairly high heat, stirring constantly, for 1 minute.

❸ Add the corn and mangetouts, and stir them over a moderate heat for 5–8 minutes, or until evenly cooked.

❹ Mix together the sherry vinegar, honey and soy sauce, and stir into the pan with the sunflower seeds. Season with pepper to taste. Cook, stirring constantly, for 1 minute. Serve the sauté hot with rice or with Chinese egg noodles.

extremely easy

serves 4

5–10 minutes

10 minutes

COOK'S TIP

Rice vinegar or balsamic vinegar make good substitutes for sherry vinegar.

Skewered Spicy Tomato Chicken

INGREDIENTS

*500 g/1 lb 2 oz skinless,
   boneless chicken
   breasts*
3 tbsp tomato purée
2 tbsp clear honey
*2 tbsp Worcestershire
   sauce*
*1 tbsp chopped fresh
   rosemary*
*250 g/9 oz cherry
   tomatoes*
*sprigs of rosemary, to
   garnish*
couscous or rice, to serve

❶ Using a sharp knife, cut the chicken into 2.5 cm/1 inch chunks and place in a bowl.

❷ Mix together the tomato purée, honey, Worcestershire sauce and rosemary. Add to the chicken, stirring well to coat evenly.

❸ Alternating the chicken pieces and tomatoes, thread them onto eight wooden skewers. Spoon any remaining glaze over the threaded skewers.

❹ Cook under a preheated hot grill for 8–10 minutes, turning occasionally, until the chicken is thoroughly cooked. Serve on a bed of couscous or rice, and garnish with sprigs of rosemary.

 extremely easy

 serves 4

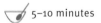 5–10 minutes

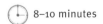 8–10 minutes

COOK'S TIP
Cherry tomatoes are ideal for barbecues because they can be threaded straight onto skewers. They remain whole, so the skins prevent the tomatoes' natural juices from seeping away.

Warm Salad of Tuna & Tomatoes with Ginger Dressing

INGREDIENTS

50 g/1¾ oz Chinese
   leaves, shredded
3 tbsp rice wine
2 tbsp Thai fish sauce
1 tbsp fresh ginger root,
   shredded finely
1 garlic clove, chopped
   finely
½ small red bird-eye
   chilli, chopped finely
2 tsp soft light brown
   sugar
2 tbsp lime juice
400 g/14 oz fresh tuna
   steak
sunflower oil for
   brushing
125 g/4½ oz cherry
   tomatoes
fresh mint leaves and
   mint sprigs, roughly
   chopped, to garnish

❶ Place a small pile of shredded Chinese leaves on a serving plate. Place the rice wine, fish sauce, ginger, garlic, chilli, brown sugar and 1 tablespoon lime juice in a screw-top jar, and shake well to combine the ingredients evenly.

❷ Cut the tuna into strips of an even thickness. Sprinkle with the remaining lime juice.

❸ Brush a wide frying pan or griddle with the oil and heat until very hot. Arrange the tuna strips in the pan and cook until just firm and light golden, turning them over once. Remove and set aside.

❹ Add the tomatoes to the pan and cook over a high heat until lightly browned. Spoon the tuna and tomatoes over the Chinese leaves and spoon the dressing over them. Garnish with fresh mint and serve warm.

 extremely easy

 serves 4

 5 minutes

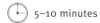 5–10 minutes

Steamed Yellow Fish Fillets

INGREDIENTS

500 g/1 lb 2 oz firm fish
   fillets, such as red
   snapper, sole or
   monkfish
1 dried red bird-eye chilli
1 small onion, chopped
3 garlic cloves, chopped
2 sprigs fresh coriander
1 tsp coriander seeds
½ tsp turmeric
½ tsp ground black
   pepper
1 tbsp Thai fish sauce
2 tbsp coconut milk
1 small egg, beaten
2 tbsp rice flour
red and green chilli
   strips, to garnish
soy sauce, to serve

 very easy

 serves 4

 10 minutes

12–15 minutes

❶ Remove any skin from the fish and cut the fillets diagonally into long 2 cm/¾ inch wide strips.

❷ Place the dried chilli, onion, garlic, coriander and coriander seeds in a pestle and mortar and grind them to a smooth paste.

❸ Add the turmeric, pepper, fish sauce, coconut milk and beaten egg, stirring well to mix evenly.

❹ Dip the fish strips into the paste mixture, then into the rice flour to coat lightly.

❺ Bring the water in the bottom of a steamer to the boil, then arrange the fish strips in the top of the steamer. Cover and steam for about 12–15 minutes, or until the fish is just firm.

❻ Garnish the fish with the chilli strips, then serve with soy sauce and stir-fried vegetables or salad.

46

Baked Cod with a Curry Crust

INGREDIENTS

½ tsp sesame oil
4 pieces cod fillet, about
   150 g/5½ oz each
85 g/3 oz fresh white
   breadcrumbs
2 tbsp blanched
   almonds, chopped
2 tsp Thai green curry
   paste
rind of 1 lime, finely
   grated
salt and pepper
boiled new potatoes,
   to serve
lime slices and rind and
   mixed green leaves,
   to garnish

 extremely easy

 serves 4

 5 minutes

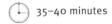 35–40 minutes

❶ Brush the sesame oil over the base of a wide, shallow ovenproof dish or tin, then lay the pieces of cod on top in a single layer.

❷ Mix the fresh breadcrumbs, almonds, curry paste and grated lime rind together, stirring well to blend thoroughly and evenly. Season to taste with salt and pepper.

❸ Carefully spoon the crumb mixture over the fish pieces, pressing lightly to hold it in place.

❹ Place the dish, uncovered, in a preheated oven at 200°C/400°F/Gas Mark 6 and bake for 35–40 minutes, or until the fish is cooked through and the crumb topping is golden brown.

❺ Serve the dish hot, garnished with lime slices and rind, and mixed green leaves, and accompanied by boiled new potatoes.

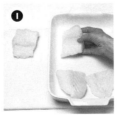

COOK'S TIP
To test whether the fish is cooked through, use a fork to pierce it in the thickest part. If the flesh is white all the way through and flakes apart easily, the fish is cooked sufficiently.

Salpicón of Crab

INGREDIENTS

¼ red onion, chopped
½–1 green chilli, deseeded
    and chopped
juice of ½ lime
1 tbsp cider vinegar or
    other fruit vinegar,
    such as raspberry
1 tbsp chopped fresh
    coriander
1 tbsp extra-virgin olive
    oil
225–350 g/8–12 oz fresh
    crab meat
lettuce leaves, to serve

TO GARNISH
1 avocado
lime juice, for tossing
1–2 ripe tomatoes
3–5 radishes

extremely easy

serves 4

10 minutes

0 minutes

❶ Combine the onion with the chilli, lime juice, vinegar, fresh coriander and olive oil. Add the crab meat and toss the ingredients together lightly.

❷ To make the garnish, cut each avocado in half around the stone. Twist apart, then remove the stone with a knife. Carefully peel off the skin and slice the flesh. Toss the avocado gently in lime juice to prevent discoloration.

❸ Halve the tomatoes, then remove the cores and seeds. Dice the flesh. Slice the radishes thinly.

❹ Arrange the crab salad on a bed of lettuce leaves, garnish with the avocado, tomatoes and radishes, and serve the salad at once.

COOK'S TIP

For a toasted crab salad sandwich, split open a long roll or a baguette and heap crab salad on it, then a layer of cheese. Grill the open roll to melt the cheese. Spread the toasted plain side with mayonnaise and close up. Cut and serve with salsa.

Fish Burritos

about 450 g/1 lb firm-
fleshed white fish,
such as red snapper or
cod
¼ tsp ground cumin
pinch of dried oregano
4 garlic cloves, chopped
finely
125 ml/4 fl oz fish stock,
or water mixed with a
fish stock cube
juice of ½ lemon or lime
8 flour tortillas
2–3 leaves cos lettuce,
shredded
2 ripe tomatoes, diced
Salsa Cruda
salt and pepper
lemon slices, to serve

 very easy

serves 4

5 minutes

45 minutes

COOK'S TIP
Cook several peeled
waxy potatoes in the
fish stock, then dice
them and serve them
wrapped in the warm
tortillas with lettuce,
fish, tomato and salsa.
Alternatively, add slices
of avocado dressed
with lime to the filling.

❶ Season the fish with salt and pepper, then put it in a pan with the cumin, oregano, garlic and enough fish stock to cover it.

❷ Bring to the boil, then cook for about 1 minute. Remove the pan from the heat and leave the fish to cool in the cooking liquid for about 30 minutes.

❸ Remove the fish from the stock and break it into bite-sized pieces. Sprinkle the cooked fish with the lemon or lime juice, and set it aside.

❹ Heat the tortillas in an ungreased non-stick frying pan, sprinkling them with a few drops of water as they heat. Wrap them in a clean tea towel when they are heated, to keep them warm.

❺ Arrange shredded lettuce in the middle of one tortilla, spoon a few big chunks of the fish onto it, then sprinkle it with the tomato. Add Salsa Cruda. Repeat with the other tortillas and serve at once with lemon slices.

Cod Curry

INGREDIENTS

1 tbsp vegetable oil
1 small onion, chopped
2 garlic cloves, chopped
2.5 cm/1 inch piece fresh
    ginger, roughly chopped
2 large ripe tomatoes,
    skinned and roughly
    chopped
150 ml/5 fl oz fish stock
1 tbsp medium curry paste
1 tsp ground coriander
400 g/14 oz canned
    chickpeas, drained
    and rinsed
675 g/1 lb 8 oz cod fillet,
    cut into large chunks
4 tbsp chopped coriander
4 tbsp natural yogurt
salt and pepper
steamed basmati rice,
to serve

❶ Heat the oil in a large saucepan and add the onion, garlic and ginger. Fry for 4–5 minutes, or until the ingredients are softened. Remove from the heat. Put the onion mixture into a food processor or a blender with the tomatoes and fish stock, and blend until smooth.

❷ Return to the saucepan with the curry paste, ground coriander and chickpeas. Mix together well, then simmer gently for 15 minutes, or until thickened.

❸ Add the pieces of fish and return to a simmer. Cook for 5 minutes, or until the fish is just tender. Remove from the heat and leave to stand for 2–3 minutes.

❹ Stir in the coriander and yogurt. Season and serve with steamed basmati rice.

 easy

 serves 4

 10 minutes

 30 minutes

Barbecued Monkfish

INGREDIENTS

4 tbsp olive oil
grated rind of 1 lime
2 tsp Thai fish sauce
2 garlic cloves, crushed
1 tsp grated fresh ginger
    root
2 tbsp chopped fresh
    basil
700 g/1 lb 9 oz monkfish
    fillet, cut into chunks
2 limes, each cut into
    6 wedges
salt and pepper

❶ Mix together the olive oil, lime rind, fish sauce, garlic, ginger and basil. Season and set aside.

❷ Wash and dry the fish. Add to the marinade and mix well. Leave to marinate for 2 hours, stirring occasionally.

❸ If you are using bamboo skewers, soak them in cold water for 30 minutes. Then lift the monkfish pieces from the marinade and thread them onto the skewers, alternating with the lime wedges.

❹ Transfer the skewers to a lit barbecue or to a preheated ridged grill pan. Cook for 5–6 minutes, turning regularly, until the fish is tender. Serve immediately.

 extremely easy

 serves 4

 10 minutes,
plus 2 hours to
marinate

 5–6 minutes

Stuffed Mackerel

INGREDIENTS

4 large mackerel,
   cleaned
1 tbsp olive oil
1 small onion, finely
   sliced
1 tsp ground cinnamon
½ tsp ground ginger
2 tbsp raisins
2 tbsp pine nuts, toasted
8 vine leaves in brine,
   drained
salt and pepper

❶ Wash and dry the fish and set it aside. Heat the oil in a small frying pan and add the onion. Cook gently for 5 minutes, or until softened. Add the cinnamon and ginger, and cook for 30 seconds before adding the raisins and pine nuts. Remove from the heat and allow to cool.

❷ Stuff each of the fish with a quarter of the stuffing mixture. Wrap each fish in 2 vine leaves, securing with cocktail sticks.

❸ Cook on a preheated barbecue or a ridged grill pan for 5 minutes on each side, or until the vine leaves have scorched and the fish is tender. Serve immediately.

 very easy

 serves 4

 10 minutes

 12 minutes

Prawn & Asparagus Risotto

1.2 litres/2 pints
    vegetable stock
350 g/12 oz asparagus,
    cut into 5 cm/2 inch
    lengths
2 tbsp olive oil
1 onion, chopped finely
1 garlic clove, chopped finely
350 g/12 oz arborio rice
450g/1 lb raw king
    prawns, peeled and
    deveined
2 tbsp olive paste or
    tapenade
2 tbsp chopped fresh basil
salt and pepper
Parmesan cheese,
    to garnish

❶ Bring the vegetable stock to a boil in a large saucepan. Add the asparagus and cook for 3 minutes, or until just tender. Strain, reserving the stock, and refresh the asparagus under cold running water. Drain and set aside.

❷ Heat the oil in a large frying pan, add the onion and cook gently for 5 minutes, or until softened. Add the garlic and cook for an additional 30 seconds. Add the rice and stir for 1–2 minutes, or until coated with the oil and slightly translucent.

❸ Keep the stock on a low heat. Increase the heat under the frying pan to medium and begin adding the stock, a ladleful at a time, stirring well between additions. Continue until almost all the stock has been absorbed. This should take 20–25 minutes.

❹ Add the prawns and asparagus with the last ladleful of stock, and cook for an additional 5 minutes, or until the prawns and rice are tender and the stock has been absorbed. Remove from the heat.

❺ Stir in the olive paste, basil and seasoning and leave to stand for 1 minute. Serve immediately, garnished with Parmesan shavings.

easy

serves 4

10 minutes

45 minutes

John Dory en Papillote

INGREDIENTS

2 John Dory, filleted
1 cup stoned black olives
12 cherry tomatoes,
    halved
115 g/4 oz green beans,
    topped and tailed
handful fresh basil
    leaves
4 slices fresh lemon
4 tsp olive oil
salt and pepper
fresh basil leaves,
    to garnish
boiled new potatoes,
    to serve

❶ Wash and dry the fish fillets and set aside. Cut 4 large rectangles of baking paper measuring about 45 × 30 cm/ 18 × 12 inches. Fold in half to make a 22.5 × 30 cm/9 × 12 inch rectangle. Cut this into a large heart shape and open out.

❷ Lay one John Dory fillet on one half of the paper heart. Top with a quarter of the olives, tomatoes, green beans, basil and one lemon slice. Drizzle 1 teaspoon of olive oil over the top, and season the dish well with salt and pepper.

❸ Fold over the other half of the paper and fold the edges of the paper together to enclose. Repeat to make 4 packets.

❹ Place the packets on a baking sheet and cook in a preheated oven at 200° C/400° F/Gas Mark 6 for 15 minutes, or until the fish is tender.

❺ Transfer each parcel to a serving plate, unopened, allowing your guests to open their packets and enjoy the wonderful aroma. Suggest that they garnish their portions with fresh basil, and serve a generous helping of boiled new potatoes onto each plate.

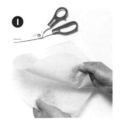

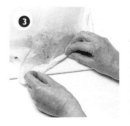

 very easy

 serves 4

 15 minutes

 15 minutes

Salads
&
Side
Dishes

People are generally aware that most salads are composed of low-fat ingredients, but it may be a surprise to find such delicious combinations as in this section. Tuna Bean Salad is a fresh tuna steak on a bed of beans in a lemony olive-oil dressing – a medley of flavours. For an unusual side dish, try Fideos Tostados, a dish of rice and very thin pasta cooked together in a tomato sauce. Jasmine Rice with Lemon and Basil has a refreshing fragrance.

Jasmine Rice with Lemon & Basil

INGREDIENTS

200 g/7 oz jasmine rice
400 ml/14 fl oz water
rind of ¼ lemon, finely grated
1 tbsp fresh sweet basil, chopped

❶ Wash the rice in several changes of cold water until the water runs clear. Bring the water to the boil in a large pan, then add the rice.

❷ Bring back to a boil. Turn the heat to a low simmer, cover the pan, and simmer for an additional 12 minutes.

❸ Remove the pan from the heat and leave it to stand, covered, for 10 minutes.

❹ Fluff up the rice with a fork, then stir in the lemon. Serve scattered with basil.

 extremely easy

serves 4

5 minutes, plus 10 minutes' standing

20 minutes

COOK'S TIP

It is important to leave the pan tightly covered while the rice cooks and steams inside so that the grains cook evenly and become fluffy and separate.

Thai-style Carrot & Mango Salad

INGREDIENTS

4 carrots
1 small, ripe mango
200 g/7 oz firm tofu
1 tbsp fresh chives,
    chopped

DRESSING
2 tbsp orange juice
1 tbsp lime juice
1 tsp clear honey
½ tsp orange-flower
    water
1 tsp sesame oil
1 tsp sesame seeds,
    toasted

❶ Peel the carrots and grate them roughly. Peel and stone the mango, and slice it thinly.

❷ Cut the tofu into 1 cm/½ inch cubes and toss together with the carrots and mango in a wide salad bowl.

❸ For the dressing, place all the ingredients in a screw-top jar and shake well to mix evenly.

❹ Pour the dressing over the salad and toss well to coat the salad evenly.

❺ Just before serving, toss the salad lightly and sprinkle the chives over it. Serve immediately.

 extremely easy

 serves 4

 10 minutes

⏲ 0 minutes

COOK'S TIP
A food processor will grate the carrots in seconds, so it is a useful time-saving device if you are catering for a large number of people.

68

Tuna Bean Salad

 very easy

 serves 4

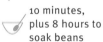 10 minutes,
plus 8 hours to
soak beans

 2 hours

❶ Soak the white kidney beans for 8 hours or overnight in at least twice their volume of cold water.

❷ When you're ready to cook, drain the beans and place in a saucepan with twice their volume of fresh water. Bring slowly to the boil, skimming off any scum that rises to the surface. Boil the beans rapidly for 10 minutes, then reduce the heat and simmer for an additional 1¼–1½ hours, or until the beans are tender.

❸ Meanwhile, mix together the lemon juice, olive oil, garlic and seasoning. Drain the beans thoroughly and mix together with the olive oil mixture, onion and parsley. Season to taste and set aside.

❹ Wash and dry the tuna steaks. Brush them lightly with olive oil, and season. Cook on a preheated ridged grill pan for 2 minutes on each side until they remain just pink in the centre.

❺ Divide the bean salad between 4 serving plates. Top each with a tuna steak. Garnish with parsley sprigs and lemon wedges, and serve immediately.

COOK'S TIP
You could use canned navy beans instead of dried. Reheat according to the instructions on the can, drain, and toss with the dressing as described above.

70

Spiced Lentils with Spinach

INGREDIENTS

2 tbsp olive oil
1 large onion, chopped finely
1 large garlic clove, crushed
½ tbsp ground cumin
½ tsp ground ginger
250 g/9 oz Puy lentils
600 ml/1 pint vegetable
   or chicken stock
100 g/3½ oz baby
   spinach leaves
2 tbsp fresh mint leaves
1 tbsp fresh coriander leaves
1 tbsp fresh flat-leaved
   parsley leaves
freshly squeezed
   lemon juice
salt and pepper
grated lemon rind,
   to garnish

 easy

 serves 4

 10 minutes

35 minutes

❶ Heat the olive oil in a large frying pan over a medium–high heat. Add the onion and cook for about 6 minutes. Stir in the garlic, cumin and ginger, and continue cooking, stirring occasionally, until the onion just starts to brown.

❷ Stir in the lentils. Pour in enough stock to cover the lentils by 2.5 cm/1 inch and bring to the boil. Lower the heat and simmer for 20 minutes, or according to the instructions on the packet, until the lentils are tender.

❸ Meanwhile, rinse the spinach leaves in several changes of cold water and shake dry. Chop the mint, coriander and parsley leaves finely.

❹ If no stock remains in the pan, add a little extra. Add the spinach and stir through until it just wilts. Stir in the mint, coriander and parsley. Adjust the seasoning, adding lemon juice and salt and pepper. Transfer to a serving bowl and serve, garnished with lemon rind.

COOK'S TIP

This recipe uses green lentils from Puy in France because they are good at keeping their shape even after long cooking. You can, however, also use orange or brown lentils, but time them according to the cooking instructions on the packet or they will turn to a mush.

Courgettes & Tomatoes with Green Chilli Vinaigrette

INGREDIENTS

1 large fresh mild green chilli, or a combination of 1 green pepper and ½–1 fresh green chilli
4 courgettes, sliced
2–3 garlic cloves, chopped finely
pinch sugar
¼ tsp ground cumin
2 tbsp white wine vinegar
4 tbsp extra-virgin olive oil
2–3 tbsp coriander
4 ripe tomatoes, diced or sliced
salt and pepper

❶ Roast the mild chilli, or the combination of the green pepper and chilli, in a heavy-based ungreased frying pan or under a preheated grill until the skin is charred. Place in a plastic bag, twist to seal well and leave the mixture to stand for 20 minutes.

❷ Peel the skin from the chilli and pepper, if using, then remove the seeds and slice the flesh. Set aside.

❸ Bring about 5 cm/2 inches water to the boil in the bottom of a steamer. Add the courgettes to the top part of the steamer, cover and steam for about 5 minutes, or until just tender.

❹ Meanwhile, combine the garlic, sugar, cumin, vinegar, olive oil and coriander thoroughly in a bowl. Stir in the chilli and pepper, if using, then season with salt and pepper as necessary to taste.

❺ Arrange the courgettes and tomatoes in a serving bowl or on a plate and spoon the chilli dressing over them. Toss gently, and serve immediately.

 easy

 serves 4

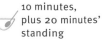 10 minutes, plus 20 minutes' standing

 10 minutes

Potatoes in Green Sauce

*1 kg/2 lb 4 oz small waxy
potatoes, peeled
1 onion, halved and
unpeeled
8 garlic cloves, unpeeled
1 fresh green chilli
8 tomatillos, outer husks
removed, or small tart
tomatoes
225 ml/8 fl oz chicken,
meat or vegetable
stock, preferably
home made
½ tsp ground cumin
1 sprig fresh thyme or
generous pinch dried
1 sprig fresh oregano or
generous pinch dried
2 tbsp vegetable or
extra-virgin olive oil
1 bunch fresh coriander,
chopped
1 courgette, chopped
roughly
salt*

❶ Put the potatoes in a pan of salted water. Bring to the boil and cook for about 15 minutes, or until almost tender. Do not over-cook them. Drain and set aside.

❷ Lightly char the onion, garlic, chilli and tomatillos or tomatoes in a heavy-based, ungreased frying pan. Set aside, and when cool enough to handle, peel and chop the onion, garlic and chilli; chop the tomatillos or tomatoes. Put in a blender or a food processor with half the stock, and process to form a purée. Add the cumin, thyme and oregano.

❸ Heat the oil in the heavy-based frying pan. Add the purée and cook for 5 minutes, stirring, to reduce slightly and concentrate the flavours.

❹ Add the potatoes and chopped courgette to the purée and pour in the rest of the stock. Add about half the coriander and cook for a further 5 minutes, or until the courgette pieces are tender.

❺ Transfer to a serving bowl and serve sprinkled with the remaining chopped coriander to garnish.

 easy

 serves 4

 20 minutes

 30 minutes

Fresh Pineapple Salsa

1 small ripe pineapple
juice of 1 lime or lemon
1 garlic clove, chopped
    finely
1 spring onion,
    thinly sliced
½–1 fresh green or red
    chilli, deseeded and
    chopped finely
½ red pepper, deseeded
    and chopped
3 tbsp chopped fresh
    mint
3 tbsp chopped fresh
    coriander
pinch of salt
pinch of sugar

❶ Using a sharp knife, cut off the top and bottom of the pineapple. Place upright on a board, then slice off the skin, cutting downward. Cut the flesh into slices, halve the slices and remove the cores. Dice the flesh. Reserve any juice that accumulates as you cut the pineapple.

❷ Place the pineapple in a bowl and stir in the lime juice, garlic, spring onion, chopped chilli and red pepper.

❸ Stir in the chopped fresh mint and coriander. Add the salt and sugar, and stir well to combine all the ingredients thoroughly. Chill until ready to serve.

 extremely easy

 serves 4

 15 minutes

 0 minutes

Fideos Tostados

INGREDIENTS

350 g/12 oz vermicelli or
    angel hair pasta in
    coils, roughly broken
100 g/3½ oz long-grain
    white rice
3 tbsp extra-virgin olive
    oil
200 g/7 oz canned
    chopped tomatoes,
    drained
600 ml/1 pint chicken
    stock or water, plus
    extra if necessary
1 bay leaf
1–2 tsp chopped fresh
    oregano or 1 tsp dried
    oregano
½ tsp dried thyme leaves
salt and pepper
1–2 tbsp sprigs and
    chopped fresh
    oregano or thyme,
    to garnish

❶ Put the pasta and rice in a dry, large, heavy-based saucepan or flameproof casserole over a medium-high heat, and cook for 5–7 minutes, stirring frequently, until light golden. (The pasta will break unevenly, but this does not matter.)

❷ Stir in 2 tablespoons of the olive oil, together with the chopped tomatoes, stock, bay leaf, oregano and thyme, then season with about 1 teaspoon of salt and pepper to taste.

❸ Bring to the boil, reduce the heat to medium and simmer for about 8 minutes, stirring frequently, to help unwind and separate the pasta coils.

❹ Reduce the heat to low and then cook, covered, for about 10 minutes, or until the rice and pasta are tender and all the liquid is absorbed. If the rice and pasta are too firm, add about 125 ml/4 fl oz more stock or water and continue to cook, covered, for an additional 5 minutes. Remove from the heat.

❺ Using a fork, fluff the rice and pasta into a warmed deep serving bowl and drizzle with the remaining oil. Sprinkle with the herbs and serve immediately.

very easy

serves 4

5 minutes

30–35 minutes

Desserts

With a little thought (and discipline) it is possible to create a low-fat dessert that looks and tastes wonderful. Espresso Granita is ice flavoured with coffee or vanilla, served in chilled bowls. It is fat-free, yet it makes a perfect end to a meal. Chocolate & Raspberry Vacherin is an impressive dessert for a special occasion, a low-fat meringue layered with melted chocolate and crème frâiche, and there is a reduced-fat Chocolate Mousse. Fruit is an equally delicious but less indulgent alternative. In the following pages it is combined imaginatively with potato in Fruity Potato Cake, and with pasta in Raspberry Fusilli.

Lychee & Ginger Sorbet

INGREDIENTS

800 g/1 lb 12 oz canned lychees in syrup
rind of 1 lime, finely grated
2 tbsp lime juice
3 tbsp stem ginger syrup
2 egg whites

TO DECORATE
starfruit slices
slivers of stem ginger

❶ Drain the lychees, reserving the syrup. Place the fruits in a blender or a food processor with the lime rind and juice, and stem ginger syrup, then process until completely smooth. Transfer to a mixing bowl.

❷ Mix the purée thoroughly with the reserved syrup, then pour into a freezerproof container and freeze for 1–1½ hours, or until slushy in texture. (Alternatively, use an ice-cream maker.)

❸ Remove from the freezer and whisk to break up the ice crystals. Whisk the egg whites in a clean, dry bowl until stiff, then quickly and lightly fold into the iced mixture.

❹ Return to the freezer and freeze until firm. Serve the sorbet in scoops, decorated attractively with slices of starfruit and slivers of ginger.

very easy

serves 4

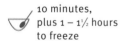
10 minutes, plus 1 – 1½ hours to freeze

0 minutes

COOK'S TIP

Raw egg whites should not be served to young children, pregnant women, the elderly, or anyone weakened by chronic illness. If you leave the egg whites out of this recipe, you whisk the sorbet a second time after another hour of freezing to obtain a light texture.

Fruity Potato Cake

INGREDIENTS

675 g/1 lb 8 oz sweet
potatoes, diced
1 tbsp butter, melted
125 g/4½ oz
demerara sugar
3 eggs
3 tbsp milk
1 tbsp lemon juice
grated rind of 1 lemon
1 tsp caraway seeds
125 g/4½ oz dried fruits,
such as apple, pear or
mango, chopped
2 tsp baking powder
brandy or rum (optional)

easy

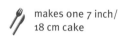
makes one 7 inch/
18 cm cake

20 minutes

1 – 1¼ hours

COOK'S TIP
This cake is ideal as a
special occasion dessert.
It can be made in advance
and frozen until required.
Wrap the cake in clingfilm
and freeze. Thaw at room
temperature for 24 hours
and warm through in a
moderate oven before
serving.

❶ Grease an 18 cm/7 inch square cake tin lightly.

❷ Cook the sweet potatoes in boiling water for 10 minutes
or until soft. Drain and mash the sweet potatoes until they
are smooth.

❸ Transfer the mashed sweet potatoes to a mixing bowl
while they are still hot, and add the butter and sugar,
mixing to dissolve.

❹ Beat in the eggs, lemon juice and rind, caraway
seeds and chopped dried fruit. Add the baking powder
and mix well. A few drops of brandy or rum may be added
at this stage, if wished.

❺ Pour the mixture into the prepared cake tin.

❻ Cook in a preheated oven, 160°C/325°F/Gas Mark 3, for
1–1¼ hours or until they are cooked through. Remove the
cake from the tin and transfer it to a wire rack to cool. When
it is cold, cut it into thick slices to serve.

Raspberry Fusilli

INGREDIENTS

175 g/6 oz fusilli
700 g/1 lb 9 oz
   raspberries
2 tbsp caster sugar
1 tbsp lemon juice
4 tbsp flaked almonds
3 tbsp raspberry liqueur

❶ Bring a large pan of lightly salted water to the boil. Add the fusilli and cook until tender but still firm to the bite. Drain the fusilli thoroughly, return to the pan, and set it aside to cool.

❷ Using a spoon, press 225 g/8 oz of the raspberries firmly through a sieve set over a large mixing bowl to form a smooth purée.

❸ Put the raspberry purée and sugar in a small saucepan and simmer over a low heat, stirring occasionally, for 5 minutes. Stir in the lemon juice and set the sauce aside until required.

❹ Add the remaining raspberries to the fusilli in the pan and mix together well. Transfer the raspberry and fusilli mixture to a serving dish.

❺ Spread the almonds out on a baking sheet and toast under the grill until golden brown. Remove and set aside to cool slightly.

❻ Stir the raspberry liqueur into the reserved raspberry sauce and mix well until very smooth. Pour the raspberry sauce over the fusilli, then sprinkle the toasted almonds generously over the top, and serve.

 easy

 serves 4

 10 minutes

20 minutes

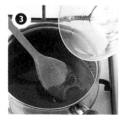

Chocolate & Raspberry Vacherin

3 egg whites
175 g/6 oz caster sugar
1 tsp cornflour
25 g/1 oz semisweet
   chocolate, grated

FILLING
175 g/6 oz semisweet
   chocolate
450 ml/16 fl oz half-fat
   crème fraîche
350 g/12 oz fresh
   raspberries
a little melted chocolate,
   to decorate

❶ Draw 3 rectangles, 10 × 25 cm/4 × 10 inches, on sheets of baking paper, and place them on 2 baking sheets.

❷ Whisk the egg whites in a bowl until they form peaks. Whisk in half the sugar gradually, then whisk until the mixture is stiff and glossy. Fold in the rest of the sugar, the cornflour and grated chocolate with a metal spoon or spatula.

❸ Spoon the meringue mixture into a piping bag fitted with a 1 cm/½ inch plain nozzle, and pipe lines over the rectangles.

❹ Bake in a preheated oven, 140°C/275°F/Gas Mark 1, for 1½ hours, changing the positions of the baking sheets halfway through. Keeping the oven door shut, turn off the oven and leave the meringues to cool inside, then peel away the paper.

❺ To make the filling, melt the chocolate and spread it over 2 of the meringue layers. Leave the filling to harden.

❻ Place 1 chocolate-coated meringue on a plate and top with about one-third of the crème fraîche and raspberries. Place the second chocolate-coated meringue on top and spread with half the remaining crème fraîche and raspberries.

❼ Put the last meringue on top, spread with crème fraîche and fruit, drizzle melted chocolate over the top, and serve.

 easy

 serves 4

25 minutes

1½ hours

Chocolate Mousse

very easy

serves 4

10 minutes,
plus 2 hours
to chill

5 minutes

❶ Put the melted chocolate, natural yogurt, Quark, caster sugar, orange juice and brandy in a food processor, and blend for 30 seconds. Transfer the mixture to a large bowl.

❷ Sprinkle the gelatine over the water and stir until dissolved.

❸ In a small saucepan, bring the gelatine and water to the boil for 2 minutes. Leave to cool slightly, then stir into the chocolate mixture.

❹ Whisk the egg whites until stiff peaks form, and fold into the chocolate mixture using a metal spoon.

❺ Line a 850 ml/1½ pint loaf tin with clingfilm. Spoon the mousse into the tin. Chill the mousse for 2 hours in the refrigerator until it is set. Turn the mousse out onto a plate, decorate it with the grated dark and white chocolate and orange zest, and serve.

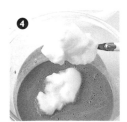

Espresso Granita

INGREDIENTS

200 g/7 oz caster sugar
600 ml/1 pint water
½ tsp vanilla essence
600 ml/1 pint very strong
  espresso coffee,
  chilled
fresh mint, to garnish

❶ Put the sugar in a saucepan with the water and stir over a low heat to dissolve the sugar. Increase the heat and boil for 4 minutes, without stirring. Use a wet pastry brush to brush down any spatters on the side of the pan.

❷ Remove the pan from the heat and pour the syrup into a heatproof non-metal bowl. Sit the bowl in the kitchen sink filled with iced water to speed the cooling process. Stir the vanilla and coffee into the syrup, and let it stand until it is completely cool.

❸ Transfer to a shallow metal container, cover and freeze. (It will keep for up to 3 months.)

❹ Thirty minutes before serving, place serving bowls in the refrigerator to chill.

❺ To serve, invert the container on a chopping board. Rinse a cloth in very hot water, wring it out, and rub it on the base of the container for 15 seconds. Shake the container sharply and the mixture should fall out. If not, repeat.

❻ Use a knife to break up the granita and transfer it to a food processor. Quickly process it until it becomes grainy and crunchy. Serve the granita at once in the chilled bowls, decorated with mint.

 very easy

 serves 4

 10 minutes, plus 2 hours to freeze

10 minutes